JOURNEY *to the* CENTER *of the*
EARTH

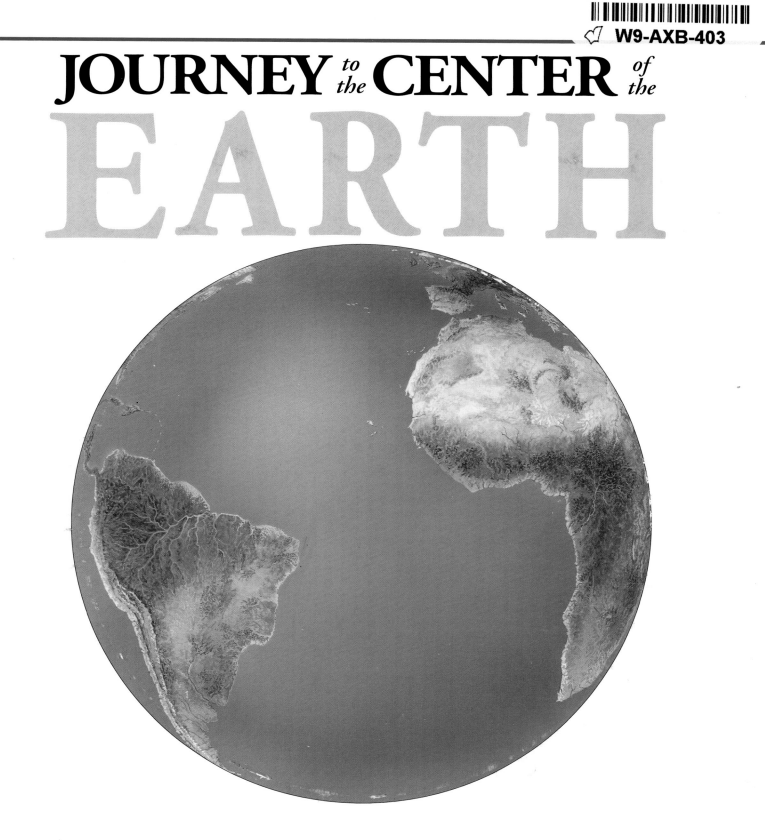

Written by Nicholas Harris
American text by Marc Gave
Illustrated by Gary Hincks

Reader's Digest Children's Books™

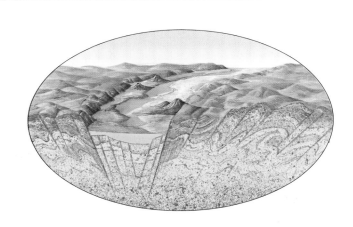

Reader's Digest Children's Books

Created and produced by Nicholas Harris, Joanna Turner, and Claire Aston, Orpheus Books Ltd

American text by Marc Gave

Illustrated by Gary Hincks

Consultants: Professor Jonathan K. Filer, Ph.D., and Susanna van Rose

Published by Reader's Digest Children's Publishing, Inc. Reader's Digest Road, Pleasantville, NY 10570-7000

Copyright © 1999 Orpheus Books Ltd

ISBN 1-57584-274-2

Library of Congress Catalog Card Number: 98-66624

Printed and bound in Singapore

◆ CONTENTS ◆

6 Watery Planet
Oceans • Ocean currents • Continental shelf • Ocean floor

8 Dynamic Earth
Continental drift • Tectonic plates • Subduction zones • Mountain building • Earthquakes • Mid-oceanic ridge • The Earth's internal layers

11 Atmosphere
Layers of the atmosphere • The Sun's rays

12 Clouds
What clouds are made of • Why it rains • Different cloud types • The water cycle

14 Plants and Animals
Food chains and webs • Nutrient cycle • Photosynthesis

16 Soil
What soil is made of • Soil fertility • Layers of the soil • Microscopic life

18 Surface Rocks
Minerals • Sedimentary rocks • Erosion •
Limestone • Caves • Fossils

20 Crust
Folding and faulting • Jewels •
Metamorphic rocks

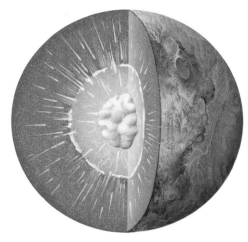

22 Upper Mantle
Magma • Igneous rocks • Volcanoes

24 Lower Mantle
Heat flows • Earthquake waves

26 Outer Core
Liquid metal • The Earth's magnetic field

28 Inner Core
Meteorites • Origin of the Earth

30 Glossary

31 Index

◆ INTRODUCTION ◆

How deep have people traveled into the Earth? Not very deep—just 2.5 miles (4 km). They have dug holes up to 9 miles (15 km) deep, but that's still only a very short way compared to the great distance—almost 4,000 miles (6,400 km)—to the center of the Earth.

What has kept us from going deeper? For starters, there's miles and miles of solid rock. Even if we could get through that, we'd encounter intense heat—so much heat that it can melt rock. And even if we had suits that could protect us from the heat, nothing could protect us from the tremendous pressure at the Earth's core.

Not being able to travel very deep hasn't stopped scientists from studying the inside of the Earth. By using special instruments, they have learned much about the Earth's inner layers.

And it's the knowledge these scientists have gained that makes the imaginary journey you are about to take possible—a journey to the center of the Earth.

When two continental plates collide, they tend to squeeze together and buckle up into mountain ranges. The best example of this is the Himalayas, formed when the Indian Plate rammed into the Eurasian Plate.

Most *earthquakes* occur where plates collide or slide past one another, such as along the San Andreas Fault in California. The plates may lock together, causing pressure to build up. When the plates suddenly give, intense energy is released and shock waves are sent out in all directions.

▶ These cross sections show the difference between the rocks that make up the continents *(upper circle)* and the ocean floors *(lower circle)*. Continents are complicated masses of rocks that are much older than ocean rocks. Beneath the ocean sediment lie volcanic rocks that have cooled in the shapes of pillows and columns.

Sediment

Ocean floor

Mid-oceanic ridge

See inset, right

Molten rock rises to the surface

Convection currents (see page 24)

▼ All along a mid-oceanic ridge, molten rock rises from inside the Earth. As it emerges into the cold water, it cools rapidly and becomes solid. The more molten rock that oozes out, the more the ocean floor spreads apart. This happens at about the same speed as your fingernails grow.

Ocean floor

Mid-oceanic ridge

Molten rock rises

• DYNAMIC EARTH •

THINK OF THE EARTH as a kind of machine with moving parts. Nothing stays the same. Not even the vast landmasses we call the continents have always been where they are today. Over hundreds of millions of years, they have drifted across the globe while the oceans have widened or narrowed. Millions of years ago the continent of South America, for example, fit snugly into the west coast of Africa.

How does this happen? Like a jigsaw puzzle, the Earth's surface is divided into about 15 jagged-edged pieces called *tectonic plates*. The plates are always shifting, although too slowly for us to notice. When an ocean plate collides with a continental plate, the edge of the thinner, denser ocean plate slides beneath the continental plate. This process is called *subduction*, and the place where an ocean plate slides down is called a subduction zone.

▼ In a subduction zone, as the ocean floor sinks, a deep trench forms. At great depths the rocks eventually melt. Some of this melted, or molten, rock rises, erupting at the surface as volcanoes. A subduction zone runs nearly all the way around the Pacific Ocean. There are so many volcanoes that it is called the Ring of Fire.

Molten rock rises

Volcano

Continental shelf

Trench

Sea level

Abyssal plain

Seamount

Ocean floor

Continent

Subduction zone

A *mid-oceanic ridge* is actually a series of smaller ridges separated by cracks that run at right angles to the ridges.

◆ WATERY PLANET ◆

BEFORE we begin our journey, let's take a look at planet Earth as a whole. Imagine we are out in space, with the Earth spinning before our eyes. We would see what looks like a giant beach ball, mostly blue with white streaks, and two white patches. The white streaks are clouds floating just above the surface, while the white patches are regions of ice covering the North and South Poles. The blue areas covering more than two-thirds of the Earth's surface are the oceans. The Earth is the only planet in the solar system that has liquid water.

Beneath the ocean surface lies an amazing world that includes mountain ranges and towering *volcanoes*. But the ocean floor mostly consists of a vast plain, called the *abyssal plain*. On average it's about 3 miles (5 km) deep, although some *ocean trenches* plunge to more than twice that depth.

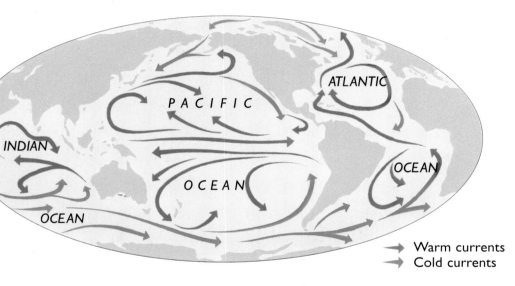

◀ The ocean waters swirl around the Earth. Warmed by the Sun, surface waters flow from the warm tropics toward the freezing poles, while cold currents move in to take their place. Winds that blow over the ocean currents carry the warm or cool temperatures to nearby lands.

→ Warm currents
→ Cold currents

▶ The steep *continental slope* marks the boundary between ocean and continent. Rivers flowing to the ocean carve deep canyons into the slope. The *continental shelf*, that part of a continent lying under water, is where most ocean life is found. The dark, near-freezing waters of the deeper oceans have far fewer inhabitants.

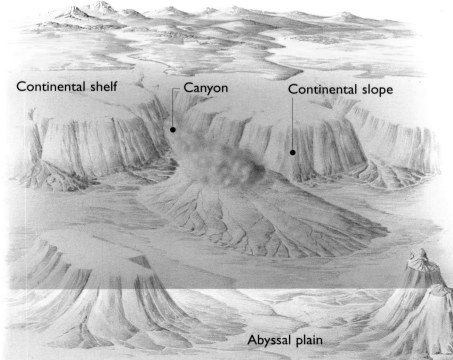

Continental shelf   Canyon   Continental slope

Abyssal plain

Unfold these pages and look right down through all the Earth's layers to its inner core.

ARCTIC OCEAN

EUROPE

NORTH AMERICA

AFRICA

Continental shelf

Continental slope

Mid-Atlantic Ridge

ATLANTIC

Seamounts

OCEAN

◄ This is what the floor of the North Atlantic Ocean would look like if all its water were drained away. Snaking down the middle is the Mid-Atlantic Ridge, a long mountain range. *Seamounts* (underwater mountains) rise from the abyssal plain. When they are high enough to break the ocean surface, they form islands.

Abyssal plain

SOUTH AMERICA

◆ CLOUDS ◆

W E ARE now in the lowest layer of the atmosphere, where the Earth's weather occurs. Winds blow and clouds form in this layer. Clouds may appear anywhere from the ground up to about 12 miles (20 km) in tropical areas. They are made up of three basic shapes: cumulus (heaped), stratus (layered), and cirrus (feathery).

Clouds form when water vapor—water that has *evaporated* (become a gas) from the Earth's surface—*condenses* (turns into a liquid). This happens when the air cools, for example, after it has been driven upward over higher ground. The water vapor condenses around tiny particles in the air such as dust or sea salt. When the air temperature is below the freezing point of water, the water droplets turn to ice crystals. If the droplets or crystals grow heavy enough, they fall as precipitation, such as rain or snow.

This is the view we normally have of clouds—looking up at them. The blue sky is our view of the atmosphere and beyond, lit by the Sun.

▼ Clouds consist of water droplets, ice crystals, or both. Snowflakes are made up of thousands of ice crystals.

Water droplet

Ice crystal

Types of Clouds

Cirrus

Cirrostratus

Cirrocumulus

Altostratus

Altocumulus

Cumulonimbus

Cumulus

Stratus

The Water Cycle

In the water cycle, water circulates from the Earth to the sky and back again. Warmed by the Sun's heat, water evaporates from the Earth's surface and oceans. The moist air is carried upward by winds, where it cools and condenses to form clouds. Eventually, water falls back to Earth as rain or snow. In very cold areas, snow may turn to ice and stay frozen for years. In other areas, rain seeps into the ground and feeds the streams and rivers that flow to the oceans.

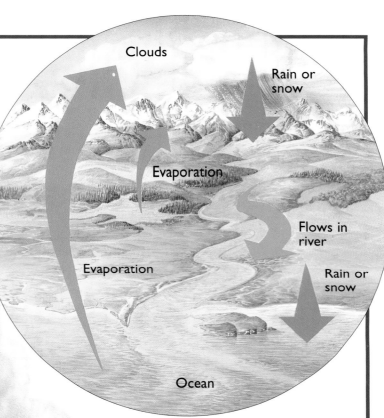

Clouds

Rain or snow

Evaporation

Flows in river

Evaporation

Rain or snow

Ocean

▲ This diagram shows the water cycle. The formation of dew is a water cycle in miniature. During the day, water evaporates from the ground. On clear nights, the ground cools, water vapor in the nearby air condenses, and tiny droplets of dew form.

Our journey continues on the next page when we land on the ground and meet some of the plants and animals that live there.

◆ PLANTS AND ANIMALS ◆

PERHAPS as many as 20 million species of plants, animals, and other living things—such as bacteria and fungi—share our planet. Living things all depend on one another for survival. Plants provide food for plant-eating animals, which become prey for flesh-eating animals. They in turn might be eaten by larger flesh-eaters. This is called a food chain. Since animals eat more than one kind of food, many food chains link together to make a food web.

Living things depend on one another in other ways, too. After they die, their bodies decay (break down). Small soil creatures *(see pages 16–17)*, including insects, worms, and tiny forms of life called microorganisms, turn this decaying material into *nutrients*. Plants need these nourishing substances in order to grow.

This is the view a ground-dwelling woodland creature might have of the world above—the underside of the tree branches and leaves.

▼ This is a diagram of a food web in a North American forest. Plant-eating animals such as rabbits are prey for lynx or bears. Shrews are insect-eaters and they are hunted by these same predators. Bears also feed directly on plants and insects. *(Arrows point toward feeder or predator.)*

Lynx
Rabbit
Bear
Shrew
Insects
Hawk
Songbird

Plants also make their own food from water, air, and sunlight. Their leaves trap the Sun's rays and take in carbon dioxide gas from the air—some of which is exhaled by humans and other animals. Meanwhile, their roots draw up water and nutrients from the soil. Then, in a chemical reaction called *photosynthesis,* the leaves produce sugars from these ingredients. Oxygen, a gas which is released in this process, is essential for humans and other animals to breathe.

▲ Nutrients are always being recycled in nature. Animals eat plants (1). The animals' waste and decaying, dead bodies (2) are turned into nutrients by microorganisms (3). Plants take nutrients up from the soil through their roots (4).

◆ SOIL ◆

OUR TRIP through the soil takes up just the first few yards (meters) of our journey to the center of the Earth. The soil layer may be thin, but it is vital to humans. Most plants would not grow without it. In turn, neither plant-eating animals nor animals that feed on them would exist. That includes us.

Everybody knows what soil looks like. But do you know what it is made of? It consists of tiny fragments of rock mixed with decaying plant and animal matter. Water and air fill the spaces between the soil particles. Also in the soil, but too small for us to see, are microorganisms, busy feeding on the decaying matter. In any handful of topsoil, there are more than ten billion of these tiny creatures.

Not all soil is the same. Soil is thicker on level ground, thinner on slopes. The climate (warm or cool, wet or dry), the kinds of plants that grow in the soil, and the kinds of rocks

Plants and animals (see pages 14–15) live in the soil as well as above ground. In any soil, you are likely to find a dense tangle of plant roots and a maze of tunnels built by animals.

▶ This illustration *(circle below)* is a greatly magnified view of plant roots in the soil. Besides anchoring plants firmly in the ground, roots absorb water and nutrients from the soil. The

that lie beneath it are some of the important factors that determine how fertile soil is.

As we tunnel through the soil, we can make out different layers. First, there is the topsoil, a layer rich with organic matter, including plant roots and animal life. Lower down, we reach the subsoil, where there are more rock fragments. As we go deeper, the fragments are larger and more frequent—until we arrive at solid rock.

Topsoil

Root

Subsoil

Rock

▲ This slice through the soil shows its different layers. Soil is full of animal life. Moles, spiders, insects, and worms are easy to spot, but most soil creatures are too small to see.

◆ SURFACE ROCKS ◆

SURFACE ROCKS form the top layer of the Earth's *crust.* Rocks lie beneath soil, city streets—even the oceans. Sometimes they lie right at the surface.

Made of chemical substances called *minerals,* rocks are formed in three different ways. We'll come across *igneous rocks* and *metamorphic rocks* later on our journey. *Sedimentary rocks* are made up of fragments of other rocks that have been broken down by the weather. Fragments worn away by wind, water, or ice in a process known as *erosion* may eventually settle on a stream bed or at the bottom of the sea. These sediments include sand, gravel, mud—even the remains of living creatures. If the sediments lie undisturbed for several million years, the grains will begin to stick together and eventually form rock. Sandstone, shale, and limestone are types of sedimentary rocks.

▼ *Fossils* are the remains of once-living things that have turned to stone. When this ammonite died (1), the soft parts rotted away, leaving the hard shell. The remains were buried by sediments under water (2). The original minerals of the shell were replaced by those in the water. Millions of years later, the sedimentary rock layer was uplifted by land movement (3). Erosion exposed the fossil (4).

Limestone (illustrated below) is made of the remains of tiny plants and animals that lived in shallow seas millions of years ago. Larger *fossils* of coiled-shell ammonites are common in this rock. Water seeps into the cracks that crisscross the limestone, and eventually widens them into caves. The seeping water may also form icicles of rock called stalactites on the cave ceiling. Stalagmites are built up on the cave floor when water containing dissolved limestone drips from the ceiling.

▲ Every natural landscape is altered by erosion. Eroded rock fragments are taken from highland places by wind, water, or ice and laid down

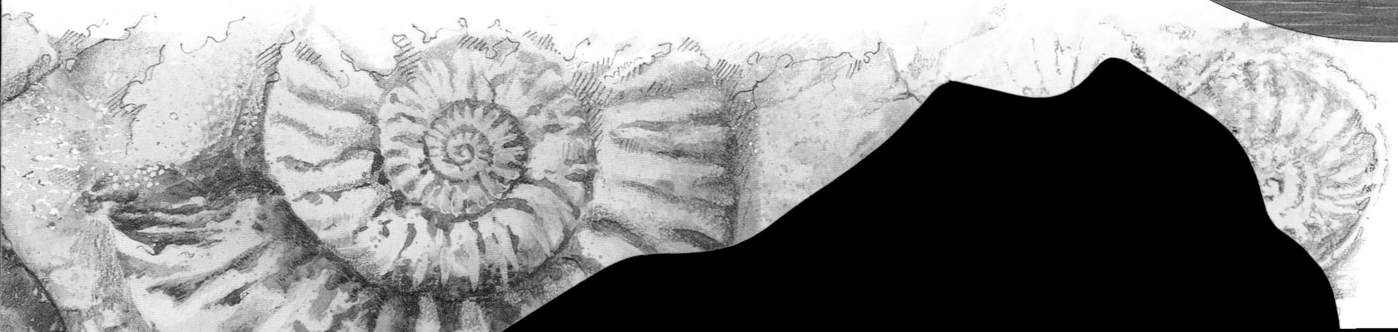

◆ CRUST ◆

ON AVERAGE, the crust takes up the first 19 miles (30 km) of our journey into the interior. Here the rocks are constantly being pressed together or cracked apart. Sometimes they fold up—like a rug on the floor if you push both ends together—and sometimes they split along cracks, called *faults*. An example of *folds* are the Alps in Europe, while the Great Rift Valley in east Africa is a gash in the Earth's crust caused by land slipping between faults. All this moving about takes millions of years, so we never notice—except when there is an earthquake.

Where two pieces of continent are forced together, the land can be pushed up to great heights. The rocks are squeezed so tightly that they begin to change. Intense heat—temperatures in the lower parts of the crust are about 2,700°F (1,500°C)—also produces changes in the rocks. This could happen in a

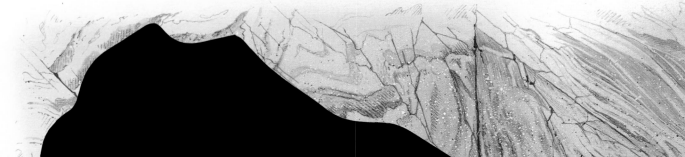

These crustal rocks have been squeezed and cracked. Cooled molten rock (the purple areas) has come into the crust from the mantle.

subduction zone *(see page 8)*, or where hot, molten rock—*magma*—from the *mantle* rises up into the crust.

When rocks change in this way, we say they metamorphose. Sedimentary rocks, igneous rocks, or even other metamorphic rocks may all undergo metamorphism. Among the kinds of metamorphic rocks are marble (originally limestone), slate (originally mudstone), and quartzite (originally sandstone).

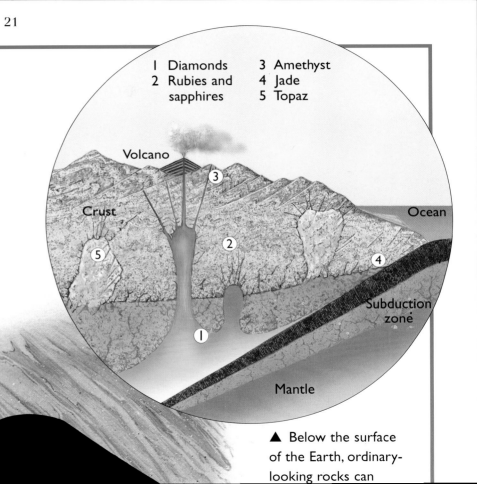

1 Diamonds
2 Rubies and sapphires
3 Amethyst
4 Jade
5 Topaz

Volcano

Crust

Ocean

Subduction zone

Mantle

▲ Below the surface of the Earth, ordinary-looking rocks can

◆ UPPER MANTLE ◆

WE'VE REACHED one of the major boundaries inside the Earth. Here we pass out of the crust into the mantle. Rocks in the upper mantle are made up of both solid, regular-shaped forms known as crystals and molten (liquid) rock lying between the crystals. It is from this crystal "mush" that magma rises into the crust, sometimes bursting out at the Earth's surface.

Magma bubbles up through the crust in subduction zones *(see page 8)*. Water from the wet sediments on the ocean floor makes the magma more runny, so it rises through cracks in the crustal rocks. The magma seeps into the rocks, sometimes building up into huge masses. It may stay there, eventually cooling down to become igneous rock. Granite is a type of igneous rock that is formed when magma

The upper mantle consists of rock crystals with molten rock between them. The temperature

beneath the Earth's surface cools very slowly.

Sometimes the magma erupts at the surface in a volcano. In some violent eruptions, the volcano shoots many millions of tons of *lava,* ash, and dust high into the air. There are also gentler eruptions, such as the ones that occur along *mid-oceanic ridges (see pages 8–9).* In those eruptions, magma bubbles up and cools quickly, producing basalt, another kind of igneous rock.

Main vent

Crater
Side vent
Ash and
lava layers

Magma

▲ Lava is magma that has erupted from a volcano. When the magma is thick and pasty, lava and gas explode in a violent eruption. This cross section of an active volcano (one that erupts frequently) shows the layers of

◆ LOWER MANTLE ◆

A S WE GO DEEPER, the temperature continues to rise. At this depth, pressure from the enormous weight of the layers above ensures that lower mantle rocks are completely solid.

It is difficult to think of a lump of solid rock ever flowing like a liquid, but over millions of years that's exactly what happens inside the mantle. Warm rock rises up through the mantle, then fans out sideways when it reaches the base of the crust. Eventually, it cools and sinks through the mantle again. At the base of the lower mantle, it heats up again, and the cycle repeats itself. These flows are called *convection currents*. They appear to play an important role in moving the tectonic plates *(see page 8)* on their seemingly never-ending journey around the surface of the globe.

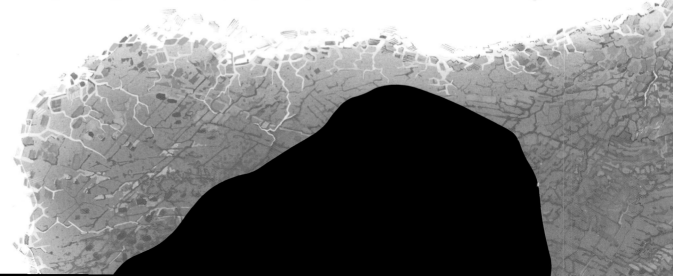

▼ Heat flows through the mantle in giant circles. As the heated rock rises and fans off in different directions, the ocean floor at the Earth's surface is gradually spread apart. Cooler rock sinks down into the depths of the mantle. Eventually, the

Probing the Earth's Interior

Earthquakes can tell us a lot about the interior of the Earth. Quakes send out vibrations, or waves, in all directions. Some waves travel through the body of the planet, but at different speeds depending on which of the various layers they pass through. By measuring these speeds, scientists have been able to calculate where, for example, the boundaries lie between the crust and the mantle, and the mantle and the *core*.

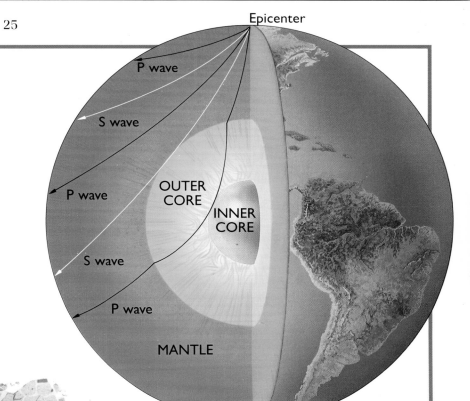

▲ In an earthquake, different kinds of waves travel outward from the focus, the place inside the Earth where rocks break or move. (The epicenter is the point on the surface above the focus.) Scientists use

◆ OUTER CORE ◆

WE'RE NOW crossing the second major boundary inside the Earth, that which lies between the mantle and the core. Suddenly, after our long journey through the mantle, there is a complete change. We are surrounded by extremely hot liquid—the only completely liquid layer inside the Earth. The material is much denser and heavier than that of the mantle. It is almost entirely metal, consisting chiefly of iron, with a small amount of nickel.

The Earth's Magnetic Field

An area that surrounds a magnet is called its magnetic field. The Earth itself has a magnetic field, as if there were a giant bar magnet

The outer core is made chiefly of iron. At temperatures rising from 7,200°F (4,000°C) to 10,000°F (5,500°C) near the boundary with the inner core, the outer core is liquid.

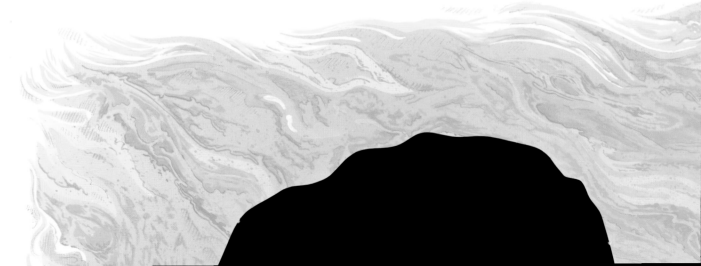

buried inside it. Scientists believe that the Earth's magnetic field is created by forces produced in the outer core. The iron in the outer core is not itself magnetic—no material will stay magnetic at these extremely hot temperatures. Convection currents *(see page 24)* are responsible for moving the liquid metal around. The currents are twisted into spiral "rollers" as the Earth spins around. They make electricity that, in turn, creates the Earth's magnetic field.

Magnetic force lines

Earth

N

S

▲ The area around any magnet is called its magnetic field. Invisible lines of force run from one pole to the other. The Earth's magnetic field stretches far out into space, making a giant teardrop shape *(below)*. It acts like a shield, protecting us from high-energy particles that stream

◆ INNER CORE ◆

AT THE CENTER of the Earth lies a solid ball of iron and nickel. Here the pressure is several million times greater than at the surface, enough to make liquid iron turn solid even at temperatures of up to 13,500°F (7,500°C).

A good way to find out about the inside of our planet is to study extraterrestrials. Not strange alien beings, but *meteorites,* fragments of asteroids—small, planet-like bodies in space—that have fallen to Earth.

Some asteroids have the same interior layers as those of the Earth, and meteorites are fragments of these various layers. Meteorites mostly made of iron, for example, probably came from asteroid cores, while other kinds may have come from the mantles or crusts.

Why does the Earth have a metal core and a rocky mantle? The Earth was formed 4.6 billion years ago. At first, our planet was extremely hot and consisted mostly of magma. Iron, a heavy metal, sank slowly through the

The Earth's inner core is made of closely packed crystals of iron with a small amount of nickel. From the center of the core, the surface lies nearly 4,000 miles (6,400 km) away.

▼ This sequence

magma to form the planet's core. Lighter *silica*-rich magma rose upward to form the rocks of the Earth's upper layers: the mantle and the crust.

We've now reached the end of our journey. What was your favorite part of the trip? What surprised you the most? Someday there may be instruments that can let us see actual pictures of what's going on inside the Earth as it's happening. For now, we can draw on what scientists have already learned and use our own imaginations to visit an incredible place where no one has ever gone.

Magma

Iron droplet

Earth's surface

CORE

Iron blob

Iron ponds

▲ This is probably what the inside of the Earth looked like as it formed billions of years ago. Iron droplets sank through the thick layer of magma just below the crust. The droplets collected into iron ponds. Then they sank further as large blobs that collected in the center as the core.

INNER CORE
4,000 miles
(6,400 km)

(3) The rocky bodies start to collide with one another, eventually building up into the planets.

(2) The dust gradually clumps together and forms fragments of rock. These grow into larger and larger blocks. The gas at the center of the disk becomes the Sun.

3

◆ GLOSSARY ◆

Abyssal plain A flat region of the ocean floor, covered by a thick layer of mud and other sediments.

Atmosphere The blanket of gases surrounding the Earth that enables life to exist.

Condensation The process by which a gas becomes liquid.

Continental shelf The part of a continent that lies beneath ocean waters.

Continental slope The steep part of the continental shelf that plunges down to the abyssal plain.

Convection currents The continual movement (flow) of a substance as it heats up and rises, then cools and sinks, then heats up and rises again.

Core The innermost portion of the Earth.

Crust The thin, rocky outer layer of the Earth. There are two main types of crust: continental and oceanic.

Earthquake A shaking or trembling of the ground, caused by the sudden movement of part of the Earth's crust.

Erosion The wearing away of the Earth's surface by water, ice, or wind.

Evaporation The process by which a liquid becomes gas.

Fault A crack in the Earth's crust, along which there is movement of one side relative to the other. Faults usually occur in rigid rocks, which tend to break rather than bend.

Fold A bend or buckle in rock caused by intense pressure. Folds usually occur in elastic rocks, which tend to bend rather than break.

Fossil The ancient remains or traces of a once-living thing, usually found preserved in rock.

Igneous rock A type of rock formed from magma that has cooled and hardened.

Lava Magma that has reached the Earth's surface through volcanoes or fissures.

Magma Hot melted, or molten, rock that is formed mainly in the Earth's upper mantle, but also deep in the crust.

Mantle The layer of the Earth that lies between the crust and outer core.

Metamorphic rock A rock that has changed due to intense pressure or heat. Metamorphic rocks can form from igneous rocks, sedimentary rocks, or even other metamorphic rocks.

Meteor A mass of rock or metal that has entered the Earth's atmosphere, often forming a streak of light as it burns.

Meteorite A meteor that reaches the surface of the Earth.

Mid-oceanic ridge A long mountain range under the ocean, where magma rises to the Earth's surface.

Mineral A natural chemical substance that is neither plant nor animal. Rocks are made up of minerals. Minerals are the most common solid material found on the Earth.

Nutrient A vital chemical substance that all living things need to live and grow.

Ocean trench A long, narrow, deep valley in the ocean floor.

Photosynthesis The process by which green plants use sunlight, water, and carbon dioxide to make their food. All animals use oxygen, a waste product of this process, to breathe.

Seamount An underwater mountain that is formed by volcanic eruptions.

Sedimentary rock A type of rock that is formed by the pressing together of rock fragments and/or the remains of living things.

Silica A compound of silicon and oxygen, silica is found in most of the minerals that make up the Earth's crust and mantle.

Subduction The process by which the edge of one crustal plate slips beneath another. The place where this occurs is called a subduction zone.

Tectonic plates The large slabs into which the Earth's surface is divided. The plates move relative to one another in a process called plate tectonics, which helps explain the theory of continental drift.

Volcano An opening in the Earth's crust through which magma erupts. The name is usually used to describe a cone-shaped mountain with a central vent and a crater at the summit.

Water cycle The process by which water circulates from the land or oceans to the atmosphere and back again.